LAURINE'S VOICE

A Garden of Poetry

By Laurine R. Blackson-White

ISBN 978-1-329-08681-4 90000
9 781329 086814

DEDICATION

This volume of poetry was written by my mother, Mrs. Laurine R. Blackson-White. I found them one day in some old paperwork. I decided there was no greater tribute I could pay to her than to surprise her on Mother's Day with a published copy of her very own exquisite work. Happy Mother's Day, Mom!

All My Love,
Ruth

Beauty

God created beauty,
And I see it in the trees.
All of nature's beauty
Seems so much a part of me.

I see it in the birds
And the yellow bumblebee.
All the four-legged creatures –
Even bugs that scare me!

I love to watch the snake
As it wiggles with ease,
Winged creatures in flight
As they float on the breeze.

If I could just caress them –
An expression of my love
I would feel like as a lowly human,
I'd reached out and touched God.

Have you ever stopped for a moment
And seriously looked
At all the marvelous beauties
Right underneath your foot?

Walk through the meadows –
Gaze through the trees –
There are many beautiful things
You haven't taken time to see.

If you only stop for a moment
To concentrate and see –
In your moments of depression
You would feel much more at ease.

In this complicated world
Full of stress and strain,
The enjoyment of God's beauty
Can be enjoyed without the pain.

So very few have seen it.
O, what an untold shame!
Each time you take a look
There is always some little change.

Can you see the beauty?
Spring, summer, winter, fall
Each season as it changes –
There is beauty in them all.

God blessed us with mountains
And many babbling brooks.
Hills, valleys, rivers, lakes, seas, and
oceans too!

God created all this beauty
Just for
Me
And
You!!!!

Mama

I stand atop an oak tree
Looking down into the grass,
Remembering Mama on her knees
Long ago – in the past.

It could have been my Mama
Grandma or great-grand,
A little bit of each one
Went into my making from God's hand.

Through their trials and tribulations
They looked through the trees,
Enduring all the hardships
While down on their knees.

They sang their songs of woes
The melodies lingered in the trees
They were picked up by the wind
And carried with the breeze.

They plotted in their minds
How to ascend from this depth
Because deep in their hearts
They knew what was best.

Their melodious music kept them on track.
While inspiring in their children
The many things they lacked
As they toiled in the soil bending their backs.

Mama aspired to higher heights
And she knew the road was long
God gave her inspiration
That was projected in her song

She sang in the grass,
Lifted her eyes to the trees,
She thought about the sky
As far as she could see

I've made it to the treetop
Which is higher than some hills.
Martin Luther King, Jr.
Spoke of the mountains
And dreams - his hopes and life's perils

We have ascended life's ladder
But there are many rungs to go –
Segregation, discrimination, prejudice,
And racial hatred are still a major foe

Many challenges confront us
Wherever winds may blow.
It won't always be easy
Sometimes progress will be slow

We've gotten to the treetops
So, take your children by the hand
Point them to the mountains
And continue Mama's plan.

Let there be no limit –
Keep Mama's dreams alive.
Let's keep going forward,
Expanding our dreams beyond the sky

Our roots grow deep,
They extend far and wide
Through the grasses in the fields
And up the mountainside

There are many more goals to achieve—
We can do it!
Let's remember Mama,
And put our minds to it.

How Did They Know?

I sneaked into my parent's room,
I knew I shouldn't do it.
The fact it was a "no-no!"
Added lots of pleasure to it.

I gazed through mischievous eyes
Upon their made-up bed,
And decided to play acrobat
Doing flip-flops over my head.

Boy, I had a ball –
It was a lot of fun.
I jumped, I tumbled, I rolled and laughed.
Wow! I had just begun.

I invited my brother and sister
To come and join the fun.
They rolled and leaped a little,
And then said that they were done.

Fear crept into their eyes –
They began to think:
What happens if they find out?
We'll all be in the clink!!

What party poopers those two were!
How could they be so dumb?
Mama wasn't smart enough
To know what we had done.

I jumped a little higher
I kicked up both my heels,
I leaped and danced with glee.
Oh, boy what a thrill!

Then it happened,
Much to my surprise.
I heard a loud noise
Pop!!!! Crack!! Crunch!!
On the other side!

I timidly got down
To see what stopped my fun.
Doggone! The bed's leg broke!
Now my fun is done.

Would they know the difference?
I decided – No, neither one.
They would flop on their bed tonight
Then say, "Oh, no! What have we done?"

I threatened my brother and sister.
I gave them such a fright.
I promised what I'd do to them
If they told on me that night.

I had the bases covered - lots of fun too.
I forgot the broken bed.
I was lost in all the many thoughts
Wandering through my head.

That night as I lay quietly in my bed
Anticipating sleep,
I suddenly heard a string of curse words
That were loud, long and deep.

It came to me suddenly then –
I could see it in my mind:
My daddy in his underwear
On the floor – and in the air: his behind.

How I whooped and hollered
And laughed till it hurt my sides.
I couldn't stop laughing,
I giggled until I cried.

Then came the moment
That was a great surprise.
Mama called us all downstairs
And stood us side by side.

She said, "I know who did it!"
I'm giving you a chance.
Let the guilty one speak up
Without a song and dance.

Quiet filled the room.
A hush was in the air.
The others all looked downcast
For they knew this wasn't fair.

"Laurine, you did it!
"I know it was you.
"You probably threatened the others
"If they told what they knew."

How could she know –
Know it was me?
There must have been a camera
Hidden somewhere I didn't see.

The Call

It sounded from the rooftops,
Vibrated in the steel,
It echoed down the alleys,
And bounced off windowsills.

The beat needs re-establishing,
The message sent far and wide,
It's time to rekindle
A united people's pride.

Where is the united feeling
We use to speak about?
Has the city overwhelmed us
While we struggled in this fight?

Have the new opportunities
Gone to our head?
All the troubles in the past
Tucked under a forgotten bed.

Do you think we have reached a plateau
Where we can afford to quit
Building stairways for our children?
Yet our struggles we forget!

Lift up your heads, young brothers!
And all you sisters too!
The battle has just begun
Don't rest, you've got work to do!

The call has been resounding.
Choose your battle stations, stand tall
The fight is tough
And we need you one and all.

Are the reefers taking over?
What about the drink, the coke,
The speed, the pills?
Whatever causes your thrill.

Is it really worth the effort?
Can you really bear the lost?
Do you want to be blank-headed?
Have you considered the cost?

You are such beautiful children
It makes God cry and me too!
That drugs, alcohol, and partying
 are your destruction
Because you didn't stop or think or do.

You are your people's assets.
You are more valuable than pure gold.
Without you as a commodity
The story can't unfold.

The drums have begun to beat again.
Your time is running out.
You think we'll give you up
Without a serious fight?

Come to us
Let's join hands and unite.
As we develop our heritage
With long-range success in sight,

Look down the dirty alleys,
Search the many rooftops,
Check in basement windows,
We have to look nonstop.

Reach out to our lost children
Let's all try and give a hand.
Each one is very special
To our Master, our God's plan.

The call has been revitalized,
Echoing down city streets,
Unite, hold hands in brotherhood,
And all march to the beat!!

Cora

Cora's door is always open,
Her heart is open wide.
We've always found joy
And a lot of love inside.

She has traveled life's highway
With determination and pride,
Striving for her family
Knocking barriers aside.

Cora delivered four children
Into this diversified world.
With her wisdom and perseverance
They survived many perils.

There is Ruth the brain,
Laurine the athlete,
Estella the thinker,
And David, the lone fellow.

They cried, hollered, kicked
And screamed.
But Cora set her goal
And pushed for a dream.

All educated, honest, independent, and
self-motivated.
We thank God above that she is still here.
All Cora's children are doing fine.
And spreading her love, she fills us with
cheer.

Her love is everlasting memories
Cherished through the years.
She surpasses the highest mountains,
And the blades of grass in fields near.

Should she ever have to leave us,
Let it be known today,
That she will always be revered
As we go our numerous ways.

Let it also be noted
As I speak out today, Cora will always be
For if there is me,
There is she.

The Candy

Daddy had a box of candy
Hidden in his dresser drawer.
He gave us each a piece last night
But I knew that there was more.

Mama is in the kitchen.
Daddy is down the street.
I'll have just one more piece,
I'll be a little sneak!

There was about fifty pieces,
But now there's only one.
Daddy won't know the difference,
He is really rather dumb.

"Laurine, what are you chewing?"
"Nothing Mama Dear,
"I'm thinking about eating meat,"
I declared loud and clear.

"What have you gotten into?
"Tell me what you have done!
"You're going to get in trouble you know,
"For any wrong you've done."

She doesn't know anything.
How could she say that?
Daddy is blind as a bat,
Don't know his head from his hat.

Later that night
Daddy is in a rage.
"Someone is going to get whooped.
"Somebody has misbehaved!

"Where's my candy?
"Most of it is gone!
"Someone ate it up and,
"They knew they were wrong!"

Mama lined us up.
Looked at us one by one.
She had a thoughtful look –
She knew what had been done.

"Laurine, you did it!
"I see it very clear,
"I knew you did something
"When you called me Mama Dear!"

White Elephant

Dedicated to Ruth Blackson
(April 10, 1989)

The elephant is an animal rare.
I send them to you Ruth, from me by air.
They represent a love I share –
I place them in your hands for care.

A white elephant is a sign of blessings
I wish a lot of such for you.
A special kind is what I send –
Full of love and grace until the end.

I also Ruth, send one little dime.
It is a representation of time.
And it stands for April 10th,
The special day for your presentation.

The dime stands for ten –
A number to remember when
You're down and out, feeling low.
Think of ten people that you know.

Cora, Laurine,
Estella, David, Karen,
Vernon, Ruth,
Steven, Stefani, Adrienne

These are ten people
Who hold you dear.
In their hearts,
They want you near.

Within these ten hearts, Ruth,
Is a part of you.
And in their own way,
Each loves you true.

So take this dime, Ruth,
And inside the white elephant is a place.
It represents a special space,
Where family love can be kept safe.

Each year it will be sent again.
You are to do the very same.
It will show you the love of ten,
So to you this token I will send

Hold on to the family love we share.
It's placed in your hands for care.
If you give up and let it go,
You'll break our hearts and hurt us so.

Look to the white elephant
When you feel fear.
Remember the ten loves
That are always near.

Reach out,
We're just one step away.
And we'll know that you need
To see our love today.

Thank You

Dedicated To Erma Lawrence
(1989)

I like to play around with rhyme –
I do this in my extra time.
So in this rhyming state of mind,
I write a note – a "thank you" kind.

I say thank you, dear friend.
You kept me going when
I wanted to give up, let go,
Of the dream I had and wanted so.

Your radiant smile,
Your special glow,
The encouragement you gave,
Saying, "Don't let go!"

You were there from the start.
You got me through the hardest parts.
You reminded me, "I have gone that route
"I know the headaches – what it's all
about."

The push you gave, got me through,
The hints of things I should do.
You unselfishly gave, when you had time.
The help you gave was the important kind.

To say thank you, is one small part
Of the gratitude that is in my heart.
You did what you didn't have to do,
And said, "I'm glad to be of help to you."

I'll remember you always,
You are kind and true.
I just wanted to express
A big THANK YOU!!!!

Hey, Daddy!

Get out of the sand,
Walk in the cement.
Did you ever give a thought
To what each footstep meant?

Stop for a moment,
Reflect upon yourself,
Which way are you going?
Does it make for success?

You are now a daddy
Do you know what that means?
You have a life in your hands
You help mold and shape dreams.

You are a creator.
It's a very special chore.
Are you ready to deal With
What life has in store?

You're the guardian of their fate –
You are the guiding light:
A parent, a friend, a counselor.
In a young child's life.

Are you man enough to finish
What you have now started?
Or, are you just a sporing plant
That will with the wind be parted?

You speak of depression,
You complain about the man.
You want to do something?
You want to have a plan?

Use your head – be intelligent.
You've got the Master's plan.
The basic foundation from you
To your child's hand.

You want to build skyscrapers?
You want to fly to the moon?
You want to be acknowledged?
You want it all and soon!

You are moving too fast.
You got to take it slow.
Start with your footprints in cement,
Instead of sand or snow.

You want your mark to last forever?
You want it solid underneath?
You need to develop your heritage!
Create victory, eliminate defeat.

Don’t wrap your arms around the world.
Stick with the Master’s plan.
Start spending time with your children
Take them by the hand.

Emphasize education –
It is the open door.
No excuse is good enough
Even if you are poor.

Whatever you have achieved –
They should aspire to more.
Building on your foundation
That opened up the door.

The progress may be slow
But it *is* a start.
Emphasize the Master’s plan
In walks through the park.

Put them on a swing
And let them soar up high.
Let them experience
How it feels to fly.

Explain to them the jubilance
Of aspiring to success.
If they don’t make it all the way,
Their children will be next.

You have got to get back on track!!
You're going in the wrong direction!
Start making footsteps towards success,
And consider your children a blessing.

My Little K.K.

Many years ago,
Much to my surprise
I had a little wonder
That came from inside.

This exciting little bundle
Was my joy and pride.
She was my little K.K.
She came from inside.

I had heard about babies
Over the years.
How they cried and hollered –
The many nights of tears.

I heard about the diapers
And the many bottles too.
But what about the joy
That I was to receive through you?

The joy was indescribable.
Love could be measured by no other.
The many feelings you develop
When you first become a mother.

I had my little K.K. –
The joy of my life.
How could I protect her
From all this worldly strife?

I didn't know how to do it.
But I sure was going to try.
She was my baby K.K.
She came from inside.

Why should I have to share her?
She belongs to me.
I knew I was being selfish,
But that's how I felt you see.

I got a little better
The longer she was here.
I shared her with my family
Even though she was so dear.

I really can't believe it
But babies really grow.
What happened to baby K.K.
From many years ago?

I thought I had lost her.
But much to my surprise
The thoughts of baby K.K.
Are still in inside.

She developed in my belly.
Now she is embedded in my mind.
Each stage of life in which she grew
Is a tabloid in time.

I pull memories up at leisure –
Whatever year I choose.
I smile over the treasures
And years of misery too.

I have many pictures
To reinforce my thoughts
Of my little baby K.K.
I once thought I had lost.

You Are Beautiful

You are a beautiful person
You must know and understand it.
Your beauty is on the inside
For that is how God planned it.

The inner beauty you possess
Is one of your greatest assets.
You have to find your special field
Where you are gifted and can excel.

It won't be easy to define –
The important factor is your frame of mind.
Believing in yourself is the very first step –
Developing your mind, doing your best.

Forget about negative things
People say.
Don't let them stop you
Or, get in your way.

You have a beautiful light
To shine.
To cultivate,
To benefit mankind.

Sometimes you may feel
Down and out.
That's part of
What life is about.

It helps teach you
To be strong.
Depending on yourself
As you go along.

Learning how to conquer fear.
Dealing with and overcoming despair.
Deciding what you want to do.
Determining what is best for you.

Sometimes you may not have much help.
People you know, you cannot trust.
But everything you go through,
Someone else has gone through it too.

"It can't work," you want to say.
But try the library on any given day.
Something you read may show the way.
Stimulate your mind – not let it stray.

Abstract thinking in a quiet atmosphere
May be the factor to make things clear.
Let your mind float without fear.
The answers to things might be near.

Try taking a pencil in your hand –
Start writing about what you can.
Write about what you want to be.
Even things you want to see.

Writing need not be a poem.
What would it take to make you strong?
Write what you want to say.
Plot your course – starting today.

If you don't like to read or write,
Don't let it bother you – it's all right.
If you can talk, talk out loud!
Be it alone or in a crowd.

Your voice may be the special line
To make you think – stimulate your mind.
It may be spoken short or long,
Or, vocalize your thoughts by way of song.

If these don't help there's more to try.
Look quietly up at the sky.
Try drawing pictures in your mind.
It may surprise you what you find.

If it is not there look at your feet.
To help you overcome defeat.
They can help you walk away from harm.
If not your feet then maybe your arms.

Strong arms to work an unknown job.
To open doors, to look inside.
Your arms might lead you on the way
To something special for you today.

Take a look at each part of you.
Analyze it and see what you can do.
By looking and searching some each day,
Believing in yourself, you'll find your way.

You are a beautiful person.
First you have to understand it.
For if you believe in yourself,
You'll come highly recommended.

You are beautiful, my lost child.
Be proud, lift up those downcast eyes.
You are a very special person inside.
Believe in yourself, develop self-pride.

My Daughter

She is my daughter,
On that we agree.
She knows for a fact,
She's a part of me.

I do not know her
Inner thoughts.
I don't really know
What's in her heart.

I know she has unspoken thoughts
She keeps inside a special part.
What does she hide on the other side?
Her thoughts and what she feels inside.

Did I somehow fall short,
Conveying to her what's in my heart?
The love I feel for her each day,
As she goes about her routine way

A mother's job is so complex
We try and do our very best.
We make mistakes along the way
But we keep trying day to day.

Sometimes our children do not see
The mountains we climbed on our way,
To make them the individuals
That they are today.

They misunderstood our intent
For what our discipline was meant.
Be it right or be it wrong,
We tried to mold them, make them strong.

They only looked at one small part
And decided they hated us in their heart.
They built a wall so very high
We ask each day, "Why, oh, why?"

They do not realize who we are.
We're standing here secure and tall,
Ready to support them should they fall –
To be there for them should they call.

At some point will she understand
That good intent was my basic plan?
The many things I wanted her to see,
Trying to pass love and wisdom to her from
me.

Maybe one day, with children of her own,
The pains and joys will to her be known.
She'll better understand what I tried to do,
After she has travelled the same road too.

I hope I'll still be here
If things should go wrong.
So we can compare notes
And together, stand strong.

To help reinforce what she tries to do.
To give a second opinion, should she
choose.
Be there for her when she's down and out.
Inspire and support her to eliminate doubt.

Let her know the children she bears
May disappoint her and not even care.
But maybe one day when she least expects
They will let her know that
As their mother she did her best.

Even if things should go wrong,
The love between them will be as it ought.
They'll stand together in their hearts,
And share together their inner thoughts.

Reaching out

You want to reach out
To a love one dear.
Say from your heart,
"I still really care."

Sometimes frustration gets in our way
And keeps us from saying
What we really want to.
So we shut it inside for another day.

Communication can be a heavy chore,
Trying to bypass what inside we store.
The misunderstandings we've had in the past
Has over us all, a shadow cast.

But we still need to say
In some little way,
That love for you is a light
That won't go out or go away.

How can we do this?
It seems so hard
Getting over things
Marked on our tally cards.

We interpret our misunderstandings
In many different ways.
We can only see our side –
Feeling right about what we say.

We all are strong-headed.
We all grew up that way.
Can we put it aside?
We are getting older every day.

Let's adopt a family pact,
So we can still convey
The love we have for each other
In some small, significant way.

I have picked the ten-cent piece
To play a little part in the walk
Toward the mending of our feelings,
And to help when we can't talk.

During misunderstandings between us
When some hate is in our hearts,
Go to the other side,
Look at the other part.

The love is still there
Sometimes hard to admit.
We share a certain love
That won't go away or just quit.

When you can't reach out,
Don't know what to do,
Think of the world without them.
That will help you make a move.

Stop, give a dime.
It will help every time
To say my love for you
Is in my heart and my mind.

Misunderstandings are ordinary things,
Not an indestructible barrier
Between families or friends
Leaving a sore that never mends.

Don't wait too late,
You're dealing with fate.
They can leave this earth tomorrow
And yourself you will hate.

You will hate yourself,
And one day you'll say,
"Was the barrier so high,
"That I let it end that way?"

Take a little time,
Put aside your pride.
Don't wait too late,
And then say, "I'm sorry," after they've died.

We all have a dime
From time to time.
Use one to convey the love
In your heart and in your mind.

www.ingramcontent.com/pod-product-compliance
Ingram Content Group UK Ltd.
Pitfield, Milton Keynes, MK11 3LW, UK
UKHW041904190726
13854UKWH00003B/1086

9 781329 086814